Psalms, Hymns, and Spiritual Songs

Mikhtam Music Presents…

Psalms, Hymns, and Spiritual Songs
*

Understanding the Call to Worship

R.L. Evans

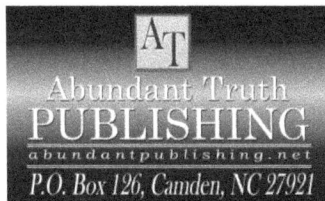

Abundant Truth
PUBLISHING
abundantpublishing.net
P.O. Box 126, Camden, NC 27921

Mikhtam Music Presents...

Psalms, Hymns, and Spiritual Songs

Understanding the Call to Worship

Cover Designs by Abundant Truth Publishing

Abundant Truth Publishing
an imprint of Abundant Truth International Ministries

For information address:
Abundant Truth International
P.O. Box 126
Camden, NC 27921

**Unless otherwise indicated, all of the scripture quotations
are taken from the** *Authorized King James Version* **of the
Bible. Scripture quotations marked with NIV are taken
from the** *New International Version* **of the Bible. Scripture
quotations marked with NASV are taken from the** *New
American Standard Version* **of the Bible. Scripture
quotations marked with Amplified are taken from the**
Amplified Bible.

ISBN 13: 978-1-60141-306-2

Printed in the United States of America

Table of Contents

Preface

I am grateful to the Lord for all He has done in my life. His wonderful works are seen daily not only in my life, but also in the life of all those that call upon His name. Because of His goodness, believers should be inspired to worship and praise His name. I have written this book to challenge and encourage others to worship the Lord in spirit and in truth.

R.L. Evans

Introduction

What is worship? What is praise and adoration? These questions remain on the frontlines of discussion in Christianity. How does one express worship, praise, and adoration in the Christian Church? Does worship consist of silence in the sanctuary? Or, is worship not worship until someone sings or lifts the hands?

In the pages of the Bible, various forms of worship are presented. Silent and vocal worship are described, as well as exuberant and clamorous forms of worship. So, which is the proper way to worship the Lord?

From the scriptures, we learn that God expects to be worshipped in many ways. There is not a set worship style that is deemed mandatory. However, one criterion does exist.

God is a Spirit: and they that worship him must worship him in spirit and in truth. (John 4:24)

God requires His worship to be offered in spirit, which could also be translated sincerity. True worship begins with a sincere heart. Alongside sincerity, truth has to be incorporated into God's worship. Worship that is not founded upon the truth of God is vain and leads men into deception.

When there is an understanding of God, Christ, and His plan for man, worship, praise, and adoration will become more than an external exercise of singing, lifting up hands, and jubilation. Worship, praise, and adoration will become the driving force in the life of the Christian.

Worship, praise, and adoration is not designed for man, but it is for the Lord. All of God's creation is endued with the responsibility and ability to worship, praise, and glorify the Lord.

Let the heavens rejoice, and let the earth be glad; let the sea roar, and the fullness thereof. Let the field be joyful, and all that is therein: then shall all the trees of the wood rejoice before the Lord. (Psalms 96:11-13a)

If all of creation praises Him, those that He has given dominion over creation have the command to worship and praise His holiness. Thus, man was created to worship, praise, and glorify Him.

This people have I formed for myself; they shall show forth my praise. (Isaiah 43:21)

The prophet declared that God called Israel unto Himself that they may praise Him. The nation existed to praise God. Since Christians become God's chosen through Jesus Christ, like Israel, they receive the same description.

> *But ye are a chosen generation, a royal priesthood, an holy nation, a peculiar people; that ye should show forth the praises of him who hath called you out of darkness into his marvelous light. (I Peter 2:9)*

The Christian's worship, praise, and adoration of God transcend the gathering together in churches. It extends into everyday life. The call to worship, praise, and adoration is not only for religious ceremonies and for assemblies, but it also has to characterize the believer's lifestyle and existence.

In this book, we will discuss the various dimensions of worship. Through the examination of biblical and religious terminology, a proper understanding of the believer's Call to Worship is established.

1

I and the Lad will go Yonder and Worship
-Genesis 22:5

The true essence of worship does not begin with religious adulations bestowed upon God. It begins with the lifestyle of those who serve Him. To understand worship, we have to look at its usage in the scriptures.

In the King James Version of the Bible, the word *worship* appears for the first time in Genesis 22. It was not used in religious service or in association with praying, singing, or the lifting of hands. Worship was used to describe an upcoming sacrifice.

And Abraham said unto his young men, Abide ye here with the ass; and I and the lad will go yonder and worship, and come again to you. (Genesis 22:5)

The Lord spoke to Abraham and commanded him to sacrifice his son Isaac. This was simply a test of Abraham's faith. When the time came for Abraham and Isaac to ascend to the place of sacrifice, Abraham makes a profound statement. He declares that the potential sacrifice (of his son) was worship. This brings us to the first component of worship.

Worship is Sacrifice

The worship of God finds its roots in sacrifice. Abraham was willing to sacrifice someone that was dear to him in order to worship.

And he said, Take now thy son, thine only

son Isaac, whom thou lovest, and get thee into the land of Moriah; and offer him there for a burnt offering upon one of the mountains which I will tell thee of. (Genesis 22:2)

Before we can enter into God's presence fully via worship, we have to be willing to give up everything first. Abraham was prepared to sacrifice what he loved for God. No one in his life would be able to compete for God's place.

If we are to experience true worship, our love for God has to supersede our love of anyone and anything else. Jesus set this standard for discipleship, which includes worship.

If any man comes to me, and does not hate his own father and mother and wife and children and brothers and sisters, yes, even

his own life, he cannot be my disciple.
(Luke 14:26)

Jesus is not instructing us to hate our families. He makes it clear that the believer must not love anyone, even himself, above God. Abraham's obedience reflects this. Before we enter into His presence with singing, the lifting of hands, and giving of thanks, we have to live a life that constitutes sacrifice and self-denial.

Then said Jesus unto his disciples, If any man will come after me, let him deny himself, and take up his cross, and follow me. (Matthew16:24)

All that will go after Christ have to deny themselves of fleshly and evil desires. The same holds true for worship. If we will go after Him in corporate and personal worship, praise, and prayer, we have to put to death the works of the flesh.

Therefore consider the members of your earthly body as dead to immorality, impurity, passions, evil desires, and greed, which accounts to idolatry. (Colossians 3:5 NASV)

Paul instructs the believers at Colossae to kill sexual immorality, moral impurity, lust, evil desires, and greediness as followers of Christ. If we hold on to these fleshly attributes, our worship and praise will be ineffective and unacceptable.

Our relationship with Christ demands self-sacrifice. Without it, the depth of worship will be limited. It may also result in rejected worship. All that we give unto God must be pure and undefiled.

I beseech you therefore, brethren, by the mercies of God, that ye present your bodies a living sacrifice, holy, acceptable unto God, which is your reasonable service. And be not conformed to this world: but be ye transformed by the renewing of your mind, that ye may prove what is that good, and acceptable, and perfect, will of God. (Romans 12:1-2)

If we walk in the aforementioned verses, our worship of God will be acceptable, effective, and meaningful. The work of preparation starts with a mind to give up all to come close to Him. We enter into true worship when we come wholeheartedly and holy. Our worship is not to be tainted by the world. Again, worship commences with sacrifice, denial, and personal holiness.

Worship is Subsistence

Worship described Abraham's potential sacrifice of Isaac. Further research reveals the depth of his statement. The Hebrew term translated *worship* means to be weighed down. Worship is to be something that an individual carries consistently.

Abraham's future descendants and God's chosen people were to be weighed down by worship; that is, they were to be worship. The use of this term equated God's people with worship. This means that the people of God not only engage in worship, but they **are** worship. From this, we discover that worship is sacrifice *and* subsistence.

Subsistence - the condition of being; condition of managing to stay alive

Worship is to characterize the believer's life and existence. The believer *is* worship. It is to be his condition or state of being. The believer recognizes that it is through the Lord that he exists and does all things.

For in him we live, and move, and have our

being; as certain also of your own poets have said, For we are also his offspring. (Acts 17:28)

The believer's life should be a living demonstration of worship. While eating, sleeping, working, and relaxing, the Lord's glory and honor should not be diminished.

Whether therefore ye eat, or drink, or whatsoever ye do, do all to the glory of God. Give none offence, neither to the Jews, nor to the Gentiles, nor to the church of God. (I Corinthians 10:31-32)

Our daily activities should bring glory and not offence to God. Our lives are to be subject to His righteousness.

In addition to being worship, the believer is to live by worship. Worship is to be the sustaining force in the believer's life. Daily, the Christian should spend time in God's presence.

Thou wilt shew me the path of life: in thy presence is fulness of joy; at thy right hand there are pleasures for evermore. (Psalm 16:11)

Worship invites God's presence into every aspect of life. The believer is worship, he lives by worship, and he is sustained by worship.

Worship is Selfless

Worship is not designed for man, but it is reserved for God alone. There is a tendency (especially seen among Pentecostal and Charismatic Christians) to believe worship is for their benefit. Though worship blesses believers, its sole purpose is to exalt and magnify the personality and power of the true and living God.

Isaiah prophetically reveals this truth,

I am the Lord: that is my name: and my glory will I not give to another, neither my praise to graven images. (Isaiah 42:8)

The Christian is to worship in appreciation and honor of God. He is not to worship with the selfish motive of receiving a blessing. God blesses us daily. Therefore, the believer's worship should not stop.

Believers should regard the opportunity to worship God as a privilege. This is because only His people are able to approach Him in worship.

Though the worship experience becomes emotional at times, it is not to be founded upon emotions. True worship is founded upon the appreciation, thanksgiving, and reverence of God. No flesh is to glory in His presence.

That no flesh should glory in his presence.
(I Corinthians 1:29)

We worship because He is worthy, not because we feel like it. If this truth is kept in mind, believers will experience God in a greater measure during their times of worship.

Remember, worship is built upon three truths: it is sacrifice, it is subsistence, and it is selfless. Without these, the worship experience will be a religious exercise rather than communion with God.

In the pages to follow, we will discuss the various dimensions of worship and praise in the religious setting. We will look at the different terms used in the worship of God.

We will also discuss the implications of them in the everyday life of believers. It is then we will be able to understand the true essence of worship.

Notes:

_____

_____

_____

_____

_____

_____

_____

_____

_____

_____

_____

_____

_____

_____

_____

2

O Come, Let Us Worship and Bow Down
-Psalm 95:6

What does it mean to worship? In the scriptures, there are numerous meanings to the word we find translated *worship*. When we understand these, we will be able to offer up to God true worship.

O come, let us worship and bow down: let us kneel before the Lord our maker. (Psalm 95:6)

True worship comes from the knowledge that God is Supreme and the Creator of all things.

He possesses all wisdom, power, and authority. Worship means to bow down or to prostrate before His greatness.

Therefore, when we say we worship God, there ought to be some actions that follow. Whether in the religious setting or in the personal lives of believers, worship requires more than a verbal declaration.

When we say that we worship God, we have to demonstrate what we are saying. If not, then our declarations are only empty words. We have to refrain from hypocrisy. We sing songs and hymns which convey the intent to worship. The only thing that is lacking is following through. Jesus warned against this type of worship when He exposed the vain worship of the people in His day.

This people draweth nigh unto me with their mouth, and honoureth me with their lips; but their heart is far from me. But in vain they do worship me... (Matthew 15:8-9a)

Our words of worship should never be vain sayings. The words of our mouths should match the intention of our hearts.

We have stated that to worship means to bow down or to prostrate. How does this occur in the religious setting? When we speak of religious setting, we mean corporate or personal settings set aside for the overall worship and reverence of God. Again, how is worship to be demonstrated after we have declared our intent through word or song?

Bowing of the Head

Regardless of the setting, when one wants to demonstrate worship, he may bow his head in reverence to God. When the head is bowed, it symbolizes that our thoughts are turned toward Him. We submit our ways unto His and our thoughts unto His because God's ways and thoughts are higher than ours.

For my thoughts are not your thoughts, neither are your ways my ways, saith the Lord. For as the heavens are higher than the earth, so are my ways higher than your ways, and my thoughts than your thoughts. (Isaiah 55:8-9)

The bowing of the head demonstrates submission unto God's purposes. It reflects our intention to submit or bow to His wisdom and word. In services, we bow our heads oftentimes when prayers are made. If we do this, we are telling the Lord that we bow our wills to His in response to our requests.

Bowing at the Waist

Depending upon the religious setting, some may feel at liberty to bow unto the Lord while in a standing position (accompanied with the lifting of hands). This type of bowing demonstrates reverence for His greatness. This type of bowing is done in respect to God as the One who fills heaven and earth.

Thus saith the Lord, The heaven is my throne, and the earth is my footstool... (Isaiah 66:1)

In Asian culture, it is customary to bow when meeting acquaintances and respecting those in authority. In the Church, we are friends and servants of God. We bow to show personal intimacy and respect.

Bowing at the waist also represents that we

set our personal desires aside to honor the Lord. This is why usually during corporate worship and personal times of devotion we do not eat, drink, and meet other physical needs to give Him our undivided attention.

Everything we have is to be submitted to Him in the act of worship. It also demonstrates that while we are in worship, we will submit any ungodly desires and appetites of the flesh unto the Lord.

Having therefore these promises, dearly beloved, let us cleanse ourselves from all filthiness of the flesh and spirit, perfecting holiness in the fear of God. (II Corinthians 7:1)

True worship will bring men and women into greater levels of personal holiness. Worship helps us to perfect holiness in the fear of the Lord.

Bending of the Knee(s)

Another common demonstration of worship is to kneel before God. Again, this is oftentimes done in connection to prayer. When possible, it should be incorporated into the worship setting. Since it involves the legs, kneeling denotes submission to God's ways. It expresses a willingness to go where He wants you to go. Your volition will be governed by His word.

The steps of a good man are ordered by the Lord: and he delighteth in his way. (Psalm 37:23)

When we kneel in the worship setting, we declare God's supremacy. We demonstrate that He alone stands in control of our lives. We submit the course and direction of our lives unto Him. We kneel to demonstrate that He is above us in authority and power.

Prostrating the Body

One of the greatest expressions of worship in the religious setting is prostration. When one prostrates, he/she is on bended knees with the face to the ground or laid out (usually face down) during the time of worship.

This act of worship denotes total surrender to the Lord. Prostration reflects a willingness to submit one's total being unto the Lord. When we do this, we declare our total trust, submission, surrender, and love.

Jesus said unto him, Thou shalt love the Lord thy God with all thy heart, and with all thy soul, and with all thy mind. (Matthew 23:27)

Those that will lay prostrate before Him in worship have to understand that this is what they are communicating. God is in control. No other will be placed before Him. His word is law. His will is unchanging.

If we are going to act this out in the worship setting, then we must be prepared to follow through. If not, we become vain worshippers.

How many times have we sang the song, *"I Surrender All"* in the worship setting? Yet, our lives do not reflect the sentiments of this song. We do not have to be perfect to sing the words to this song. However, if we are to sing it, we should be striving daily to make it a reality in our lives.

Songs like this should be meaningful outside of the religious settings. This leads us to the next area of concern. What does worship look in everyday life?

Notes:

_____

_____

_____

_____

_____

_____

_____

_____

_____

_____

_____

_____

_____

_____

_____

_____

_____

_____

_____

3

Worship in Action

In many passages of scriptures, we find the word *worship*. However, the terms used to derive the word *worship* vary in meaning in the original languages. In this brief section in our study, we will examine the various passages containing worship and their implications for the modern-day worshipper.

Bow/Prostrate to His Standards for Living

O worship the Lord in the beauty of holiness: fear before him, all the earth. (Psalm 69:9)

23

In this verse, worship means to bow and prostrate before the Lord. In everyday life, the believer worships God as He submits to His standards for living. We worship God daily when we bow to His commands.

> *For the grace of God that bringeth salvation hath appeared to all men, Teaching us that, denying ungodliness and worldly lusts, we should live soberly, righteously, and godly, in this present world. (Titus 2:11-12)*

Our reception of God's grace teaches us that true worship manifests in separation and sanctification. When we do this in our lives, we are bowing our lives in worship of Him.

Swim in (Live in) His Presence

> *Exalt ye the Lord our God, and worship at*

his footstool; for he is holy. (Psalm 99:5)

The word translated *worship* here means a pond to swim in. The psalmist is calling the people to exalt God and swim in (at) His footstool. We do this when we walk in the Spirit.

If we live in the Spirit, let us also walk in the Spirit. (Galatians 5:25)

Walking by the Spirit constitutes worship. As we allow the Spirit to lead us daily, we worship God. The only way one is able to swim is there is an abundance of water. As we are filled daily with the Holy Spirit and submit to His unction, we are in worship.

Serve the Lord in Ministry and Good Works

But this I confess unto thee, that after the way which they call heresy, so worship I the God of my fathers, believing all things which are written in the law and in the prophets. (Acts 24:14)

In his defense of the gospel, Paul stated that he worshipped the God of Israel. The word he used for worship denoted religious service. He described worship of God by faithfully ministering and serving for Him and in His name.

Thus, we worship God as we witness in His name and perform good works, which includes organized religious service.

Let your light so shine before men, that they may see your good works, and glorify your Father, which is in heaven. (Matthew 5:16)

God receives glory when we perform good works. Good works are an outward of an inner relationship. When they are done with the right motives, we worship God through them. When we serve in the Church, do volunteer work, and the like, we worship God through our actions.

True worship will come from reverence and awe of God's authority, majesty, and greatness. Worship sets God on the throne and places us at His feet. When we walk in worship, we walk in the fear of the Lord. Our fear is born out of respect for who He is. His supremacy is seen and felt throughout all creation.

Serve the Lord with fear, and rejoice with trembling. (Psalm 2:11)

If one does not respect, fear, and reverence God, the worship offered is a religious exercise only. Worship that is acceptable unto God transcends the religious setting and permeates through everyday living. When we offer this type of worship, God is exalted and we will be transformed in His presence (in or outside of the church setting). In the next chapter, we will explore the Call to Praise.

Notes:

_____

_____

_____

_____

_____

_____

_____

_____

_____

_____

_____

_____

_____

_____

4

Praise the Lord according to His Righteousness
-Psalm 7:17

"Praise the Lord!" It is one of the most common commands and declarations in the Church. What do we mean when we say it? Do we really want to give adoration and appreciation to God or is it religious talk? Do we use it to appear spiritual or righteous?

If we are going to respond properly to the call to worship, all forms of vain worship have to be forsaken. Some people use times of praise and testimony to disguise bragging about their possessions and accomplishments.

They use the name of the Lord to distract from their arrogance and pride. We have to remember that if we accomplish anything, it is because of His righteousness. Thus, he deserves a righteous praise.

I will praise the Lord according to his righteousness: and will sing praise to the name of the Lord most high. (Psalm 7:17)

David said that He would praise the Lord in proportion to His righteousness. This means that the sincerity and frequency of praise should match the depth of the Lord's righteousness. This is part of the exhortation to praise given in the last psalm. We praise God according to who He is and His works and His revealed power.

Praise him for his mighty acts: praise him according to his excellent greatness. (Psalm 150:2)

Since God is always righteous and does justly, our praise of Him should be continual. Praise should be a condition of the heart. Appreciation and thanksgiving should fuel the praise of believers. Before examining a lifestyle of praise, we want to examine the different dynamics of praise in the religious setting.

In the religious setting (corporate or personal), there are various methods used to give praise unto God. Though there are different aspects to praise, it simply means to commend and/or celebrate. When we praise God, we acknowledge His work, character, and greatness in our personal lives. In the religious setting, praise manifests in various forms.

Singing and Shouting to the Lord

One of the common ways to praise the Lord in the religious setting is in song. The exhortation to sing to the Lord is found repeatedly in the Psalms. We are challenged to come before His presence with singing.

I will praise the name of God with a song, and will magnify him with thanksgiving. (Psalm 69:30)

David declared his intent to praise God with a song. He did not sing to impress or entertain others. His songs were expressions of appreciation, adoration, and acknowledgement of God's presence in his life.

Along with singing, worshippers were instructed to shout unto the Lord. It is effective in the corporate setting if it is a part of the worship experience.

Be glad in the Lord, and rejoice, ye righteous: and shout for joy, all ye that are upright in heart. (Psalm 32:11)

When we sing in religious settings, we have to consider the words that we are singing and to whom we are singing them. We sing to exalt Him. Singing should be used in personal times of prayer and devotion.

Speaking to yourselves in psalms and hymns and spiritual songs, singing and making melody in your heart to the Lord; Giving thanks always for all things unto God and the Father in the name of our Lord Jesus Christ. (Ephesians 5:19-20)

Even if no one else enjoys our singing, the Lord will receive it when it is done to praise Him. Having a continual song in our heart should be a part of our Christian experience.

Let the word of Christ dwell in you richly in all wisdom; teaching and admonishing one another in psalms and hymns and spiritual songs, singing with grace in your hearts to the Lord. (Colossians 3:16)

Declaring the Lord's Character and Works

When we speak of the Lord's involvement in our lives, it is to be done in the context of praise. We should declare and speak of His works in our lives. This can be done with others or in times of personal devotion to encourage ourselves.

We declare His character and works through praise by bestowing adulation upon Him. It is usually expressed through using words such as bless, exalt, magnify, glorify, and exalt (all to be discussed later).

I will praise thee, O Lord, with my whole heart; I will show forth all thy marvelous works. (Psalm 9:1)

The psalmist states that his praise comes to reveal all of His marvelous works. God's works are a reflection of His character. Praise is the vehicle used to rehearse God's mighty acts and unchanging character. Praise is used to establish the works that God has done in the earth.

Knowledge of the scriptures helps us to praise God with the understanding. In the psalms, we are instructed to sing praises with the understanding.

For God is the King of all the earth: sing ye praises with understanding. (Psalm 47:7)

Knowledge of God's previous works brings a depth to our praise as we acknowledge His present work in our lives. We are to praise Him for all He has done because without His involvement in the lives of men, none would be able to stand before Him.

It is in Him that all things exist. Praise is a continual reminder of God's goodness unto us. Without His continual work in the earth, all would be lost.

O Lord, thou art my God; I will exalt thee, I will praise thy name; for thou hast done wonderful things; thy counsels of old are faithfulness and truth. (Isaiah 25:1)

Praising God for His acts of old helps to reaffirm our faith in the unchangeable God. If He did it in times of old, He will do the same for us today. This is why the psalms are full of entries remembering and praising God for His involvement in Israel's history. It encouraged the psalmist to trust God in the present difficulties.

Dancing, Clapping, and Leaping before the Lord

Dancing in praise (in religious settings) to God has increased in acceptance and popularity in recent decades. Dancing in praise to God can be choreographed or spontaneous. No matter the type, it has to be done in response to God's favor, blessing, and graciousness.

Some may argue that dancing has no place in the worship of God. However, the dance is not for us, it is for God. The psalmist encouraged the people to come before God with dancing. It was usually a sign of grateful rejoicing, pleasing to God.

Let them praise his name in the dance: let them sing praises unto him with the timbrel and harp. For the Lord taketh pleasure in his people... (Psalm 149:3-4a)

When the Ark of the Covenant came back into Jerusalem, David danced before the Lord. He chose to praise Him through dance. David played an instrument and sang. Yet, he did not choose to use either, but dance.

O Clap your hands, all ye people; shout unto God with the voice of triumph. (Psalm 47:1)

In addition to dance, some may want to leap and clap their hands in appreciation to the Lord. These can be done with or without verbal statements of praise accompanying. God interprets our actions by the intent of the heart. Thus, if we clap or dance without any verbal expressions, God will receive it as praise unto Him.

I the Lord search the heart, I try the reins, even to give every man according to his ways, and according to the fruit of his doings. (Jeremiah 17:10)

Playing Instruments

Second only to singing is the use of instruments in the praise of God. In corporate and private settings, believers use instruments to praise the name of the Lord. Instruments can be used with or without singing in the praise of God. Again, it is within the intent of the person playing that praise is offered unto God.

To shew forth thy loving kindness in the morning, and thy faithfulness every night, upon an instrument of ten strings, and upon the psaltery; upon the harp with a solemn sound. (Psalm 92:2-3)

Throughout biblical history, all manner of instruments were used to praise God. In the

Christian Church, we are to use instruments to praise Him.

Notes:

_____

_____

_____

_____

_____

_____

_____

_____

_____

_____

_____

_____

_____

_____

_____

5

The Continual Praise

How am I to praise God at all times? Am I to walk around singing and dancing all day? Am I to carry an instrument at all times to praise Him? Do I always have to be talking about something He's done to show His praises? How is the Christian to live in continual praises?

Praise God in our Conversations

I will bless the Lord at all times: his praise shall continually be in my mouth. (Psalm 34:1)

God's praise can continually be in our mouths by the conversations that we have. Though every word does not have to be a declaration of praise, our words should not distract others from God's goodness and works.

Let no corrupt communication proceed out of your mouth, but that, which is good to the use of edifying, that it may minister grace unto the hearers. (Ephesians 4:29)

The Christians' words are to be seasoned with God's grace and wisdom, which is the same as offering praise unto the Lord.

Praise God in our Appearance

In like manner also, that women adorn themselves in modest apparel, with shame facedness and sobriety; not with broided hair, or gold, or pearls, or costly array. But (which becometh women professing godliness) with good works. (I Timothy 2:9-10)

Paul gave Timothy instructions for how the women were to dress. Their outer appearance was to match their testimony in Jesus Christ. Though Paul specifically addressed the women, we know that Christian men are to be modest in their outer appearance. This helps to adorn the gospel of Christ.

When we possess a fitting outer image and good works, the gospel message is enhanced. We stated earlier that there are non-verbal ways to praise the Lord.

Our outer appearance is also a non-verbal way that we offer praise unto God for His salvation and goodness towards us.

Praise God in Fellowship

O magnify the Lord with me, and let us exalt his name together. (Psalm 34:3)

David made an appeal that praise be done corporately. We demonstrate praise and honor to God when we have fruitful fellowship with other Christians (in and outside of the religious setting).

Not forsaking the assembling of ourselves together, as the manner of some is; but exhorting one another: and so much the more, as ye see the day approaching. (Hebrews 10:25)

Today, some claim to know God and have no fellowship with others. However, if our praise is to be perfected and acceptable, we have to have fellowship and communion with others.

Our interaction is not limited to other Christians. We are to have fruitful interactions with unbelievers, which gives praise unto God. Remember Peter's words.

But ye are a chosen generation, a royal priesthood, an holy nation, a peculiar people; that ye should show forth the praises of him who hath called you out of darkness into his marvelous light. (I Peter 2:9)

It is through our godly conversation and appearance that we show forth the work of salvation in our lives to unbelievers. This is how we show forth His praises. It is through our personal witness of the work of Christ in our lives.

We are to say the right things, present ourselves the right way, and have fellowship with others in response to God's works in our lives. Our lives should be lived in praise to Him for all He has done. It is only then that our exclamation of "Praise the Lord" will have meaning.

Notes:

_____

_____

_____

_____

_____

_____

_____

_____

_____

_____

_____

_____

_____

_____

6

Bless Ye the Lord, Ye Servants of the Lord
-Psalm 134:1

One of the common hymns sang in the Christian Church is "Bless the Lord O' My Soul." The song was developed from one of the Davidic psalms. How do we bless the Lord? He is omniscient, omnipotent, and omnipresent. How then can we bless Him? Because every believer is a servant of the Lord, we demonstrate our servant-hood when we bless Him.

Behold, bless ye the Lord, all ye servants of the Lord, which by night stand in the house of the Lord. (Psalm 134:1)

47

To bless in its simplest form means to speak well of. We bless the Lord through speaking well of Him. In the Book of Revelation, John described the different accounts of how the angels and those who are in heaven bless the Lord.

Saying, Amen: Blessing, and glory, and wisdom, and thanksgiving, and honour, and power, and might, be unto our God for ever and ever. Amen. (Revelation 7:12)

Since angels are created to serve God and stand in His presence, they know how to bless the Lord in all His majesty.

And after these things I heard a great voice of much people in heaven, saying, Alleluia; Salvation, and glory, and honour, and power, unto the Lord our God. (Revelation 19:1)

We, therefore, can learn how we are to bless the Lord from their example. In the above verses, the angels used various terms to bless Him. We should incorporate them as we offer praise and blessing unto the Lord.

Let us now consider what it means to bless the Lord in corporate and personal settings.

Bless the Lord on the Knee

There are various terms frequently translated *bless* from the Hebrew and Greek. One Hebraic term means to kneel in reverence. This is the word used in the scripture below.

Thus will I bless thee while I live: I will lift up my hands in thy name. (Psalm 63:4)

In the religious setting, there are times when one kneels in appreciation of His works. While in this position of humility, we then thank Him for His power and strength. Kneeling down reveals our vulnerability to weakness, thus we trust in His strength.

Bless the with the Hands

As with praise, we use our hands to bless the Lord. Another term translated *bless* means to salute.

Lift up your hands in the sanctuary, and bless the Lord. (Psalm 134:2)

A salute is done with the hand. When we lift up one or both hands, we declare God's goodness and graciousness. It is a clear sign of honor and recognition.

We salute or recognize His authority and sovereignty in our lives. Lifting up the hands serves as a sign of acknowledgment of His superiority.

Bless the Lord with Accolades

Many words can be employed to bless the Lord. Whether in song or the giving of praise, we bless the Lord through bestowing accolades upon him

Saying with a loud voice, Worthy is the Lamb that was slain to receive power, and riches, and wisdom, and strength, honour, and glory, and blessing. (Revelation 5:12)

When we want to bless Him, the most fitting words are outlined for us, as afore-stated, in the Revelation of John. As we consider some of the words used by the angels and others in heaven, we learn how to bless the Lord with accolades.

I. He is worthy to receive power, strength, and might.

When we bless God because of His **power**; we acknowledge His ability to perform all things.

God hath spoken once; twice have I heard this; that power belongeth unto God. (Psalm 62:11)

We bless Him for His power, which is seen, in our lives. His strength is revealed in His ability to uphold all things that exist.

II. He is worthy to receive riches.

God is the Creator of all things. Thus, all things belong to Him. The earth and all its wealth and **riches** belong to Him.

The earth is the Lord's, and the fulness

thereof; the world, and they that dwell therein. (Psalm 24:1)

God not only has the riches of the world at His disposal, but He also possesses the hidden treasures (riches) of knowledge and understanding. He allows those that serve Him to understand His plan and purpose for their lives.

III. He is worthy to receive wisdom.

When we bless God for His **wisdom**, we realize that none can instruct Him or train Him. God is able to give wisdom because He is the source of wisdom. God makes those that call upon His name partakers of wisdom.

Behold, thou desirest truth in the inward parts: and in the hidden part thou shalt make me to know wisdom. (Psalm 51:6)

Blessing the Lord for His wisdom makes us candidates for His wisdom to be revealed in the decisions that arise in this life.

> *If any of you lack wisdom, let him ask of God, that giveth to all men liberally, and upbraideth not; and it shall be given him. (James 1:5)*

IV. He is worthy to receive honor.

When we honor Him, we give Him credit for all of His works. When we honor God, we bless Him for His standards and statutes.

> *For the word of the Lord is right; and all his works are done in truth. (Psalm 33:4)*

We bless the Lord as we walk in obedience to Him. Our obedience to His word reveals the honor that we have for Him as God.

If ye love me, keep my commandments. (John 14:15)

V. He is worthy to receive glory.

God's name is to be set on high among the people. We bless His name when we give Him the glory in all things.

That, according as it is written, He that glorieth, let him glory in the Lord. (I Corinthians 1:31)

When we give God glory, we are boasting in His attributes. We boast in His gift of salvation and presence in our lives through His Spirit.

Bless the Lord at All Times

David declared that he would bless the Lord at all times. Is this possible? How can we bless

55

Him at all times? Again, we do this through our lifestyles.

I will bless the Lord at all times: and his praise shall continually be in my mouth. (Psalm 34:1)

We know that in the religious setting, we kneel as a way to bless God. In our daily lives, we bless God as we walk in thanks and appreciation for all that He does for us.

One of the other words in the Hebrew translated *bless* means to extinguish. When we walk in appreciation and reflection of His goodness, we extinguish doubt, fear, and unbelief from invading our lives.

For God hath not given us the spirit of fear; but of power, and of love, and of a sound mind. (II Timothy 1:7)

Finally, we bless the Lord daily as we take brief moments to acknowledge Him in all things. This is why we pray and give thanks while eating, traveling, and working. In this manner, we can bless Him at all times. In the following chapters, we will discuss the dynamics of adoration.

Notes:

_____

_____

_____

_____

_____

_____

_____

_____

_____

_____

_____

_____

_____

_____

_____

_____

_____

_____

_____

_____

_____

_____

_____

_____

_____

_____

_____

_____

_____

_____

_____

_____

7

I will Glorify Thy Name for Evermore
-Psalm 86:12

We have discussed some valuable truths about worship and praise. Always remember that worship, praise, and adoration are valuable tools of followers of God.

From the beginning, men engaged in worship to express adoration and appreciation of the One that created them. However, worship was never left to man's personal discretion. It found its definition from the One who was to be worshipped.

God, through Moses, established the Law and gave guidelines for how they were to approach Him. God gave parameters to their worship and sacrifices. When we consider worship, we cannot decide how we want to worship, but rather how He expects to be worshipped.

From the above statements, we discover that the call to worship, praise, and adoration does not begin with religious adulations bestowed upon God. It begins with the desire of God.

To worship, praise, and adore Him properly, we must always look at God's parameters.

The earliest days of man's existence was characterized by sacrifices and offerings unto God. This was demonstrated through Cain, who brought an offering of the ground; and also by Abel who brought a sacrifice of the flock.

Worship always demanded that man gave up something that was valuable to Him. This was continued in the Levitacal system and culminating in Christ. This reveals that God's concept of worship, praise, and adoration is rooted in personal sacrifice coupled with outward expression of praise and adoration. Always keep in mind that worship, praise and adoration are to characterize the believer's lifestyle.

The focus now is to examine the words of **adoration** used in the worship of God; namely, *glorify, exalt, extol, and magnify.*

As we consider the meaning of these words in the original Greek and Hebrew languages, we will discover how we are to demonstrate these words of worship everyday. In this chapter, we will discuss what it means to glorify God and His name.

I will praise thee, O Lord my God, with all my heart: and I will glorify thy name for evermore. (Psalm 86:12)

With the examination of the Hebrew and Greek terms translated into the word *glorify,* five main meanings of the word glorify are discovered. As we explore each, we will know the true essence of what we are saying when we say that we glorify the Lord.

Glorify: *Honor, Respect, Esteem*

The first meaning of glorify is to honor, respect, or esteem. When we say that we glorify the Lord, it means that we respect Him for who He is. This is its meaning in this verse in Isaiah.

Wherefore glorify ye the Lord in the fires, even the name of the Lord God of Israel in the isles of the sea. (Isaiah 24:15)

Isaiah instructed Israel to honor and respect God in the midst of His judgment and 'fires' that were upon the nation. In the midst of every trial and test, we must remember to honor all of the attributes of God. In the Book of Malachi, God asked His people a question.

A son honoureth his father, and a servant his master: if then I be a father, where is mine honour? and if I be a master, where is my fear? saith the Lord of hosts unto you... (Malachi 1:6a)

If we are to glorify God in word and deed, it should be seen in how we relate to Him. He is our Father and deserves to be honored as such. He is a Master. We glorify Him as we serve Him in total trust and obedience.

And why call ye me, Lord, Lord, and do not the things which I say? (Luke 6:46)

We glorify Him when we esteem Him above our circumstances and situations and walk in faith. We are to esteem Him above our thoughts, opinions, and viewpoints.

Many in the Church regard God's commands, standards, and promised faithfulness as religious jargon. In times of trouble, the situation is exalted above the One who is able to change all things.

Glorify Him: *Heavy*

The second meaning of glorify is to be and/or make heavy. When we glorify God, we make Him heavy. Glorifying God makes His presence known and felt in and outside of the Church.

Ye that fear the Lord, praise him; all ye the seed of Jacob, glorify him; and fear him, all ye the seed of Israel. (Psalm 22:23

Israel glorified God as a nation when they walked in obedience. They made His presence known as they obeyed Him. Christians glorify God through our good works, holy living, and endurance of suffering in His name.

If ye be reproached for the name of Christ, happy are ye; for the spirit of glory and of God resteth upon you: on their part he is evil spoken of, but on your part he is glorified. (I Peter 4:14)

The other implication of heavy is to promote. When we promote the name of God through holy living and evangelism, we glorify God. As the Church fulfills the Great Commission, we glorify the Lord.

Go ye therefore, and teach all nations,

baptizing them in the name of the Father, and of the Son, and of the Holy Ghost: Teaching them to observe all things whatsoever I have commanded you: and, lo, I am with you always, even unto the end of the world. Amen. (Matthew 28:19-20)

Therefore, when we declare He is glorified, we are committing ourselves to live in holiness, to do good works, to endure suffering in His name, and to evangelize.

Glorify His Name: *Rest/Prepare a Habitation*

The third meaning of glorify is rest or prepare a habitation. In this sense, glorifying God is an invitation for God to make His abode with us and in us.

The Lord is my strength and song, and he is become my salvation: he is my God, and

I will prepare him an habitation; my father's God, and I will exalt him. (Exodus 15:6)

In this verse, the phrase *prepare an habitation* is the word for glorify in the literal translation. Using expressions that God is glorified says that we are preparing ourselves to be a habitation for God's presence.

What? know ye not that your body is the temple of the Holy Ghost which is in you, which ye have of God, and ye are not your own? (I Corinthians 6:19)

Since the Holy Ghost indwells the believer, we glorify God as we allow His presence to lead and guide us.

For ye are bought with a price: therefore glorify God in your body, and in your spirit, which are God's. (I Corinthians 6:20)

We glorify God as we allow His presence to fill our hearts, minds, and beings. His presence fills us as we abstain from the works and lusts of the flesh.

This I say then, Walk in the Spirit, and ye shall not fulfill the lust of the flesh. (Galatians 5:16)

We make room for Him when we forsake sin. If we want to glorify God in His fullness, it is achieved through the Spirit's presence.

Glorify the Lord: *Boast*

The fourth meaning of glorify is to boast. Boast here means to brag. We are to talk about God and what He is able to do. David reveals this type of boasting in his psalms.

My soul shall make her boast in the Lord:
the humble shall hear thereof, and be glad.
(Psalm 34:7)

This type of boasting carries the connotation of challenge. God was glorified when Elijah challenged the false prophets of Jezebel. He boasted in God's ability to consume the sacrifice.

And call ye on the name of your gods, and
I will call on the name of the Lord: and the
God that answereth by fire, let him be God.
And all the people answered and said, it is
well spoken. (I Kings 18:24)

When we glorify God, we are saying that we trust Him against the odds. The Hebrew men that were threatened with the fiery furnace demonstrated this type of boasting.

Shadrach, Meshach, and Abednego

answered and said to the king, O Nebuchadnezzar, we are not careful to answer thee in this matter. If it be so, our God whom we serve is able to deliver us from the burning fiery furnace, and he will deliver us out of thine hand, O king. (Daniel 3:16-17)

No matter what the outcome would be, they glorified God by declaring that He would deliver them from Nebuchadnezzar's hand. Regardless of what is before us, we know that God will demonstrate His power and provision.

Glorify God: *To Thirst For*

The fifth meaning of glorify is to thirst for. When we glorify His name in worship and praise, we are saying that we have a thirst for God. We desire His presence, peace, and power in our lives.

This was Jesus' request to God as He entered Jerusalem.

Father, glorify thy name. Then came there a voice from heaven, saying, I have both glorified it, and will glorify it again. (John 12:28)

Jesus wanted God's presence to be with Him as He prepared to go to His trial and crucifixion. He told the Father that He was thirsty for Him.

Blessed are they, which do hunger, and thirst after righteousness: for they shall be filled. (Matthew 5:6)

As believers, when we strive for more of God and His righteousness, we show the work of God in our lives. God receives glory as we are filled with His presence and produce righteous acts.

It is clear that saying we glorify God is more than lip service. It is a declaration that we will live to make Him glorious in the eyes of the Church and the world.

Notes:

_____

_____

_____

_____

_____

_____

_____

_____

_____

_____

_____

_____

_____

8

Exalt Ye the Lord, Worship at His footstool
-Psalm 99:5

In this chapter, we will discuss three final terms used in worship: *exalt*, *extol*, and *magnify*. All of these terms are used repeatedly in the Bible. We hear them consistently in religious settings. When we understand the nuances in their meanings, it becomes easier to answer the call to worship.

The first term that we will examine is *exalt*. In a general sense, it means to lift or raise up. In the religious sense, it means that the name, character, and works of God are to be celebrated.

Exalt has three other meanings, which will be examined now.

Exalt: *Mount Up*

The first meaning of exalt is to mount up. It conveys the act of rising above. When we say that we exalt Him, we put Him above all else. His rule and judgments has the preeminence. Isaiah reveals this meaning in his writings.

> *But the Lord of hosts shall be exalted in judgment, and God that is holy shall be sanctified in righteousness. (Isaiah 5:16)*

We exalt God daily by putting His word above all else. When we put Him first, God is mounted up above everything else in our lives.

> *But seek ye first the kingdom of God, and his righteousness; and all these things*

shall be added unto you. (Matthew 6:33)

Adhering to this scripture is how we exalt the Lord in our daily lives. We should honor Him with our best. If we say we exalt Him, it is demonstrated in putting Him at the head of our lives.

Exalt Him: *To Heave*

The next meaning of exalt in the scriptures is to heave. Heave means to bear or lift up. The following verse is written with this in mind.

Be thou exalted, Lord, in thine own strength: so will we sing and praise thy power. (Psalm 21:13)

The above reveals to us that God is exalted as praise is offered up to Him. We are to heave to the Lord praise, honor, and adoration. This is to be done in visible demonstration and declarations of worship and praise. We are to heave up thanksgiving and adulation to Him. They are to be lifted up to Him in gratitude, fear, and appreciation. David revealed this type of worship through exaltation in many of His psalms.

I will offer to thee the sacrifice of thanksgiving, and will call upon the name of the Lord. (Psalm 116:1)

David revealed that praises are to be offered (heaved) up to God as a sacrifice. Believers exalt God as they heave worship and praise up to Him.

Exalt His Name: *To Be Firm*

The third meaning of exalt that will be explored is to be firm. When this term is used, it reveals the unchangeable attributes of God. When Elihu rebuked Job and his friends, He revealed God in this context.

Touching the Almighty, we cannot find him out: he is excellent in power, and in judgment, and in plenty of justice: he will not afflict. (Job 37:23)

In this verse, the word excellent is better translated exalted (in the original language). Elihu revealed that God is exalted in power; that is, He stands firm in who He is. This means that His power, character, and attributes will not alter. In the Christian experience, to exalt God means that we declare that He will never change.

Jesus Christ, the same yesterday, and today, and forever. (Hebrews 13:8)

It reveals our trust in His character. The writer of Hebrews reveals that Christ does not change. This is the basis for why we say, *"We Exalt Thee."*

Thou art my God, and I will praise thee:

thou art my God, I will exalt thee. (Psalm 118:28)

To continue our examination of the true essence of worship, two final terms are used in honoring God: *magnify* and *extol*.

Magnify: *To Heap Up (like sheaves)*

The word, magnify, means to enlarge and make big. When we say that we magnify the Lord as His servants, it means that we stack up His praises like someone who heaps bundles of sheaves. This is what the psalmist meant in this verse.

I will praise the name of God with a song, and will magnify him with thanksgiving. (Psalm 69:30)

He declared that he would magnify God through

the giving of thanks. We magnify God when we exalt, worship, praise, honor, and give glory unto Him.

Previously, we examined the praise that the heavenly hosts gave unto God and Christ. We discover that it was multifaceted. No one word could be used to praise God effectively. When the believer incorporates different words and phrases to God, we reveal His greatness; we magnify Him.

We magnify God daily through the various ways we bring glory to His name. We stated in the previous chapter that God is glorified through our holy living, good works, our endurance in suffering, and evangelism.

When we demonstrate all of these things together, we magnify the testimony of Jesus Christ in our lives.

Extol: *Extend and Throw*

The last term in worship to be examined is extol. Its meaning is close to exalt, but it has a double meaning.

Sing unto God, sing praises to his name: extol him that rideth upon the heavens by his name JAH, and rejoice before him. (Psalm 68:4)

It means to extend the hands and throw a stone. We can combine these two meanings to say throw a stone through the extending of the hands. This is the context of its use in Psalm 68. The psalmist reveals that we can place our cares in His hand because He rides (rules and is sovereign) upon the heavens. Hence, as we extol God, we are throwing stones (casting our burdens upon Him) as we extend our hands (offer up praise to Him). Again, this double meaning reveals that to extol

God means that we recognize His power and greatness by casting our cares upon Him.

Casting all your care upon him; for he careth for you. (I Peter 5:7)

When we lift our hands to him, it is a sign of surrendering our problems and cares to him.

Many are the afflictions of the righteous: but the Lord delivereth him out of them all. (Psalm 34:19)

As we extend our hands, we release our burdens to Him as if we are throwing a stone. We extol Him by accepting His willingness to deliver us out of every test and trial.

Notes:

_____

_____

Psalms, Hymns, and Spiritual Songs

_____

_____

_____

_____

_____

_____

_____

_____

_____

_____

_____

_____

_____

_____

_____

_____

_____

_____

9

Serve the Lord with Gladness
-Psalm 100:2

Though worship requires work, it should not be burdensome to the believer. Gladness should be the foundational emotion in our worship of God. In one of the most popular psalms, David encourages the believers to serve Him with gladness.

Serve the Lord with gladness: come before his presence with singing. (Psalm 100:2)

Like the other biblical terms examined in this book, the term gladness has deeper meaning. Comprehension of this meaning will help us to truly serve the Lord with gladness.

Gladness: *Remission (of liability) or postponement of labor.*

When David exhorts the people to serve the Lord with gladness, he is telling them to serve the Lord with the understanding that they are forgiven. Also, in His presence, they will find rest.

As Christians, this verse should be a reality in our lives, fueling our worship of God. We know that in Jesus we receive the forgiveness of sins. While we are in His presence, we can find rest from our trials and tests.

Come unto me, all ye that labour and are heavy laden, and I will give you rest. (Matthew 11:28)

In addition to understanding the work of God, our worship (service) is to be offered willingly, with joy. When we praise God, it is to be done with excitement and heart-felt joy.

Serving the Lord with gladness does mean serve Him with rejoicing; that is, serve Him while rejoicing. Serve Him with joy in our hearts. We can do this because of the promises of His Word.

The True Essence of Worship, Praise, & Adoration

The true essence of worship, praise, and adoration is not found solely in the religious worship experience. They find their full expression as we demonstrate reverence for God in our everyday lives. The words that we sing and say to the Lord in the religious setting should be seen in our walk with Christ. In doing so, we will truly answer the call to worship, praise, and adoration.

Notes:

Glossary of Terms

PRAISE: sing a hymn, celebrate, group celebration, commend

WORSHIP: Israelite, prostrate, bow, to swim in, prostrate, to serve, minister to God, revere and adore

MAGNIFY: to heap up (like sheaves)

EXALT: to mount up, rise, to heave

EXTOL: hold out, extended hands, throw a stone

GLADNESS: remission (of debt) or suspension of labor

BLESS: kneel in reverence, salute, extinguish, to speak well of

GLORIFY: promote, honor, respect, rest, prepare an habitation, boast, esteem, glorious, to thirst for

Bibliography

Lockman Foundation. *Comparative Study Bible.* Zondervan Publishing House. Grand Rapids, MI, c1984

The Bible Library. *The Bible Library CD Rom Disc.* Ellis Enterprises Incorporated, (c) 1988 – 2000. 4205 McAuley Blvd., Suite 385, Oklahoma City, OK 73120. All Rights Reserved.

Encarta® World English Dictionary [North American Edition] © & (P) 2006 Microsoft Corporation. All Rights Reserved. Developed for Microsoft by Bloomsbury Publishing Plc.

www.ingramcontent.com/pod-product-compliance
Lightning Source LLC
Chambersburg PA
CBHW020513100426
42813CB00030B/3221/J